THE MAN WHO SLEEPS IN MY OFFICE

PHOENIX **POETS**

THE MAN WHO SLEEPS IN MY OFFICE

JASON SOMMER

THE UNIVERSITY OF CHICAGO PRESS

Chicago and London

JASON SOMMER is professor of English and Poet-in-Residence at Fontbonne University. He is the author of two books of poems, most recently *Other People's Troubles,* winner of the 1997 Society for Midland Authors award for poetry. He received a Writers' Award from the Whiting Foundation in 2001.

The University of Chicago Press, Chicago 60637
The University of Chicago Press, Ltd., London
© 2004 by The University of Chicago
All rights reserved. Published 2004
Printed in the United States of America

13 12 11 10 09 08 07 06 05 04   1 2 3 4 5

ISBN: 0-226-76803-1 (cloth)
ISBN: 0-226-76805-8 (paper)

Library of Congress Cataloging-in-Publication Data

Sommer, Jason.
    The man who sleeps in my office / Jason Sommer.
        p.   cm.—(Phoenix poets)
    ISBN 0-226-76803-1 (cloth : alk. paper)
    ISBN 0-226-76805-8 (paper : alk. paper)
        1. Children of Holocaust survivors—Poetry.   2. Holocaust, Jewish (1939–1945)—Poetry.   3. Loss (Psychology)—Poetry.
    4. Witnesses—Poetry.   I. Title.   II. Series.

PS3569. O6532 M36 2004
811'.54—dc22

for Bernardine

Contents

Acknowledgments

Grateful acknowledgment is made to the periodicals in which these poems first appeared:

Beloit: "Elegy"
Boulevard: "Visiting the Camp," "The Long Flight Almost Over"
The Forward: "Air Over Fire"
The Journal: "Lines, in the Reflexive"
Pleiades: "What They Saw"
River Styx: "The Man Who Sleeps in My Office"
Sewanee Theological Review: "Vision"
South Dakota Review: "The Dog I'll Never Own," "Pylon Man"
Sou'wester: "Man Aboard," "Pretty Bird"
Tikkun: "Sacrifice"
TriQuarterly: "An Origin of Prayer," "The Man at the Art House"

*

I am indebted to Allison Funk, Jane O. Wayne, and Jean Wasko for the offices of literary friendship and more, and to the anonymous editor and readers of the Phoenix Poets series.

THE MAN WHO SLEEPS IN MY OFFICE

What They Saw

In the midst of, out of the depths of, through
      the strands of wire, beneath and
          between the towers and chimneys,
while they stood roll call under
      the round stars in the earliest daylight,
          or marched out to gather or break stones,

the gaze could go to the low sun gaining,
      a few trees sun-backed, leaves aswarm,
          burning and unconsumed,
or the slender flashes of birch.
      Stronger than the fear, for moments
          at a time, a particle of will summoned

out of them, a secret willing there's no help for,
      they tell me, they who were there
          in that place, or places like it,
eyes lifted toward the hills from where
      came nothing, or following a bird
          or bird song, drawn up

to a sky without smoke—
      not the yellow autumn smoke
          of burning off the potato fields

after the harvest, not the white smoke
    of the blowing snowfall—
        spring the season most often.

A flock of a hundred and more turn
    on a single edge at once,
        slicing back and forth through the spaces beneath
the clouds, dangerous to be lost
    in it, however briefly, but someone is.
        An afternoon, straight ahead of them—

among other stick figures in tatters,
    parting those shufflers and staggerers,
        come striders in uniform:
the head of the head of the women's camp,
    a hint of the blonde pennant of her hair
        in a stray lock from under her cap.

Mengele, too, movie-star handsome,
    and beyond the sexual flutter as he
        passes through the women's barracks,
whatever his actual errand, whatever he had
    done or would do, gone for
        a trance instant in his beauty.

Even downcast eyes might find
    something in a frame of vision: the yellow
        star of one dandelion beside
the pure centrifugal burst
    of another's globe of seed,
        like a little puff of smoke.

Visiting the Camp

Prague. Prague had been the point and beauty—
one final trip together as a couple
while they would try to make a family,
the ancient squares, cobblestones and steeples,
Wenceslas, Kafka, Rabbi Loew and golem.
From the start they planned this side trip, as they called it,
by train to the site of nightmare, a pilgrimage,
the spot that he had vowed to find determined
by a detail his dark grandmother let slip
out of her general muteness on the subject:
her barrack's number in the second camp.
So they could move as quickly as they needed
through the first, on toward something further
that would make an end when they arrived.

Easy enough to have the run of the place,
no guards, guides but no guards anymore
after all, and early in the day
and so late in the summer, few tourists either,
several knots of them gathering around
guides in the parking lot, sorting by language,
about to do the stations of the camp,
to be led through the gates under the iron arch's
message concerning work.
                    Lehrspruch!—he's caught
from a guide's speech, Englishing it for her

as maxim, a word for the words above the gates.
She hears in passing, *ici les Juifs et autre*.
They filter through the others, getting started
briskly on their own but soon slow down,
taking in the weathered red brick, old trees,
the graveled path—*like a college*, she hisses—
the proportions also oddly off somehow,
not merely shrunken like some childhood locale
revisited, but far from what they thought
they'd understood from the accounts, the pictures
and films, what they'd studied, wept at—
more than wept—she had that scary time
right after graduation when she starved
herself until she stopped her period,
nearly two years till she got well again.

In summative museums out of barracks,
divided among the nations—Jews become
citizens again he notes, the names
on walls, anonymous in the photographs
with faces, suggested by the artifacts,
metonymy for absence in everything:
eyeglasses, hairbrushes, suitcases, wristwatches, dolls.
At the execution yard with its pocked wall,
and at the only intact gas chamber—
prototype for those destroyed perfections
in camp II—the signs that give the facts
also ask the visitors not to speak.
Again thou shalt not, he whispers as they pause
to read what's posted in the antechamber.
(He trembles once and swears to himself he won't
tremble. She will not cry; will not; will not.)

And so that's what we shouldn't do, she says,
they don't say anywhere what we should do.

On the empty bus, he makes no move to sit.
She stands with him, and though he stoops, straining
to see the other camp appear through the windshield,
she sees it first through the driver's-side window,
rows of fence posts cropping up so quickly,
just then aware she had expected vista.

Set down across from where the rails lead straight
into the body of the camp, they enter
and follow the west-running tracks a while,
stopping at intervals, each or together, turning
slowly more and more of a circle to view
what opens in enclosure, how the wire
has made the camp and camps within the camp,
all that right-angled space whose corridors
they'll wander like relatives searching out
a headstone. The vast tracts of barracks or
their remnants, mostly wood but also brick;
to the north so many little brick chimneys
rising out of nothing, nothing, too,
his grandmother's barracks, the number to mark
where it had been, the outline gone in grass.

The grass is too green, he says, then says a thing
he's said before—how they should sow these fields
with salt. They drift back toward the tumbled stacks
of three and four, the ash pits and memorials.
She takes his hand and keeps it as they haven't
allowed themselves to do most of the morning.
She leads them now to enter one of the stands

of birch that gave the place one of its names,
still here, she thinks, *no—of that stock: seedling
to sapling to tree and seedling to sapling to tree*.

The first naked women he remembers
seeing were bulldozed into a pit on film.
Of course the bodies of others come to mind—
how can they not?—those who were naked here
and had their flesh reft from them suddenly,
or soon, this more than fear they'll be discovered
preventing them from taking off more clothing
than they do, after they've eased to the ground.
Clothes pulled up, down, out of the way,
her pale skin shining health and strength
in the birch shadow, through his half-closed eyes
for just one moment he can't help, he pictures
everything documentary black and white.

Meanwhile, what she makes of the two of them,
husband and wife, close grown, limb and trunk
in a white grove, flashes out of Ovid:
her stray thought of lovers turned to birches,
blessed in their escape, or punished in
the impiety of their resistance to all—
living, dead, dying. Except for one
not born, whom did they not resist, clasped
together, intending the copulation as
continuance enough? Once back in Prague,
they made love every day, so that whatever
happened they would never know for sure.

Reign

The windows are open so the night is everywhere,
all indoors enclosed inside that humidor,
along with the slow drill of cicadas something else
I try to name, the sound or creature that makes the sound.
Over and over, drifting down right to the edge
of sleep, I think I've found it and jerk awake only
to find it gone

                 and me back at the black and white
movie on the television, further downstream
in the doppelganger plot: brother and darker brother,
twins maybe, certainly a dream, but someone
else's I'm almost sure, until I do dream
a moment then—and wake confused—that my father was
away at school, not just for evenings as he'd been
most of my childhood.

                 I nearly tell him since he's risen
there from a crouch, his back to me in the lamplight,
searching through the bookshelves beside the couch I drowse on
in this room that is his study in a house
I say I've come home to but never lived in.
It's I who have been away at college, though he's just been
to the night school of a dream and looks it, his night face
pale as paper, crumpled slightly, inscribed with lines
from the pillow case.

              My father has returned with a word,
not in his mother tongue, or his most fluent now,

but the one in which he had his first false name assigned
him as a schoolchild before the other names he would
assume for his avoidance of the camps and slaughter.
He's checking on a word he dreamed, he says, in Czech.
Ha! Checking Czech. Czech-English/English-Czech,
the dictionary he lifts open on one palm,
then holds arm's length away and down. The only glasses
he can find are sunglasses. He fingers through pages,
stops, tilts up his face, a small strained smile with the effort
of recollection, a man who cannot see himself.

I've worn a face like that myself, dumb in the presence
of the word I'm blind to, surrounded by chattering speakers
of another language, I'm smiling up and around me,
half aware of wanting my incomprehension
to have a pleasant expression at least, as willing then
to let the words be sounds, the sounds, a music of
a kind, as I am now unwilling to let the sound
I've heard all night at intervals and hear again
be music only: an arpeggio of a single note
fanning slowly out, thumbed on the tines of a comb—
as description, accurate, but as translation, wrong.

My father, though, is *right, yes, right enough, amazing.*
But there are pages missing from his dictionary
he says and shows me just how cleanly gone, left out
at binding, produced under the Communists of course.
Surprising, the force of disappointment in his voice,
as if the pages held a word he might still need
to win a stranger over, even beyond the moment's
deception, the charming through a checkpoint into regard.

Panováni?, reign is the word he brought back
from dream. A frog makes the sound I could not name,
sound and echo joined together, calling to others
of its kind, and the sound it makes for me I recognize
at last is a pair of stones clacking underwater
in a lake upstate, where we, myself among the other
children, are submarine, everyone signaling
with the round rocks in both hands, the first summer
most of us can stay under holding our breaths.

Robert and the Same Thought

Eighteen years after the war that mattered
most to us, to our fathers—
his in the 42nd, clerk-typist

moving east with the army
toward mine who was on the run,
dodging Germans—we were twelve

and people weren't dying
in droves just then on either side
of the question of the brotherhood

of man, anywhere in our
awareness at least, in the Bronx in 1963.
Chubby Robert and skinny me,

we had all our classes together
at Junior High School 141
except for foreign languages.

He attended always in too tight
white shirts, even his hair
bulged in its combed-back, slick-dome coif—

mine stuck up in a brush cut, butch-waxed—
his black plastic frames
the thickest sort, had lenses to match,

aquarium glass, magnified
as they swam past or stopped,
his eyes, startlingly.

We would pal around sometimes,
but I called for him more frequently
after what happened in biology

(the unit: anatomy, the lesson: nerves)
when he said what I was thinking
with oddball precision,

asking the teacher whether a nerve
could protrude from the face far enough
so fingers brushing by

would make you feel something—
like antennae, I thought—but never said
a thing about it. Ours weren't out anyway,

when we walked, Robert and I
beneath the El, beside
Optimo Cigars, Woolworth, and the jewelers

with all the radios, and we had sensation
brought directly in to us
by red-faced "Irish" boys who fell in behind

like sudden fighter planes stooping
out of cloud or sun,
out of their own histories,

literally to kick our asses up the street—
this same Robert and I, driven
by their hard hurtful shoes

on buttocks, gluteus maximus—
and anus, the stunning pain
of toe to asshole—

thinking in unison again,
associating freely
on the subject of distress

and flight, bound in the skin's
ordinary discernments:
pinch, push, blow.

My Mother Making Faces

She catered to my father, so I thought even as
a child, for what he suffered in the war, guarding
the household silence around his naps and about his gaffs
in English, in many things compliant but not all.
Kittenish then, in her late twenties still, she favored
ambush, almost public: an elevator once,
she stood turned toward my father as we reached our floor,
strangers filed out ahead, and I looked up to see
she'd assumed some dreadful mask—wild eyes bugged and rolling
above a frozen snarl—and when my father winced,
she launched a mock attack, flurrying light slaps,
shoving him back into the car—*what if I had*
an accident, what if I were left that way—
wouldn't you love me, wouldn't you love me anyway?

My mother thrilled me with her faces, terrified
me, too, with crossed eyes, distorted mouth, the gargoyle
she could get from what everyone said was beautiful.
Artists painted her. We had a portrait on
our wall, a face of hers a Frenchman made: one eyebrow
arched, the oval tilted on the neck's long stem.

So when she'd flash the witch, the maenad, the visages
were more fearsome for proximity—how small
the variation that estranges beauty, turns it
grotesque.

Yet I wanted it and wanted it over,
demanding that she do them sometimes—always she
refused, her whim alone dictated when I'd feel
the delicious flush of fear, the quick sweat prickling
my scalp, the seconds that began to seem too long
before the pleasure of the restoration to her
sane features, when suddenly she was mine again,
mine all the more because my father hated it.

An Origin of Prayer

Help me he would say,

and what voice within him
said it?
       Soft half groan
he hardly believed his,

when he lay him down
escaping from a sigh,
             those words

every night during that
time of despair—
said in a sort
of deadened calm but
weeping, too,
over and over.

For months this went on,
the sound escaping
as words
       when he lay down,
eyes closed for just
a moment, as if
something within him
needed to be roused

to address something outside
before he could sleep,
then looking
through the window
by the head of his bed
that sometimes had a piece
of moon in it.

And he found he'd gotten
into a kind of habit,
so years later
he would say it before he dropped off
to sleep, in that way,
hardly saying really,
        the words forming
themselves out of an exhalation
willy-nilly.

Even back in those bad days
in the daylight
when he felt a little better
before he really was
better he had begun to
think of it as
a clear line back
to some beginning,
the tribe's more than his own,

as much in this desperate
petitioning
as in the coinages of wonder, sky
gods thundering
and the like,

that awe which after all
starts the bargaining:
o master of rain, of wind,
vouchsafe a measure
from your bounteous power
or forbear to visit
the full measure of the bounty
of your power
upon me, upon us
and if you . . . then
I will . . . we
will . . .

    And once one
warm, close September night
the night he could have
seen the meteor shower—
had he stayed up late,
                       an
amazing thing,
the fiery evaporations
of dust in the
                outermost air.

Instead he saw, or
thought he saw
         the little
exhalation he made while
summoning his strength,
confessing his weakness,
forming those words
so vaguely addressed
as a visible shimmer

three times out of his own mouth,
a vaporous dust
                    fiery
in that weak light
in
          from the window
and was afraid.

Coming

*"I like a look of agony
because I know it's true . . ."*
— EMILY DICKINSON

This one friend admits to baring
teeth, that one howls, and most
of us are very frequently
some version of the genuine.
I myself cry out, and in the sort
of smothered cry I make, you can hear
a grief at letting go I try
to modify when I'm not alone.
The sense of constriction in the sound
is sharper with the sharper pleasure
when I'm with another, the pleasure more
intense but greater, too, the desire
in me to suppress the cry—naked
evidence of the need to let go,
coupled with some need not
to be heard in such a letting go.

Deeper than vanity or of
a deeper sort of vanity,
to fear another's knowledge of me

as a species of exposure, even
then in the midst of that cry,
that act, to feel the contending desires
to be known and unknown, so close to her
face, and she, too, making her sounds
or about to, if things are going
well, my eyes on her eyes, hers
meeting mine, clenched or open,
either of us at intervals—

and the other is blurred or blacked out
and self seems self all the more
but a little lost, not being able
to tell by sight exactly where
one leaves off and the other begins,
and so entangled in one another,
not by touch either, but still thinking
of myself enough to want to seem
attractive even in abandon,
and attractive in a way I can
imagine myself looking, a way
I might hold myself, arrange myself
to look, if I knew I could be seen.

The Man Who Stopped

A phone call he was on
his way to answering,
the book he wanted from
the other room somewhere,

he thought of as he rose
headed for the ringing,
when all the momentary
purposes were closed

midstep or rather one
step over, one unbegun.
Mid-thought, and in the very
middle or midst of life,

as that expression goes,
as we are till we aren't,
he traveled toward the hardwood
floor, slammed shut, toppled,

crashed through a table like
nothing but one who lost
the lively impulses,
resembling nothing else,

through no apparent fault.

*

Not one of his forbears,
nothing in the family,
father's or mother's side
predicted by pedigree—

no comfort for us there.
We cannot say he smoked—
he didn't, or otherwise
misused himself, so chose,

or made a choice that led . . .

*

How to be comforted?
We cannot say he wished
or never did, by fifty
he must have once or twice

wanted it over with.
It came a complete surprise,
as if he'd sprouted flame
never having heard

such awful things occurred,
although it's all the same,
knowledge or ignorance,
irrelevant as justice

within the realm of chance.
What comfort in any of this
except the fact he lived
at least that first occasion?

The table that broke his ribs
started him again,
or so a doctor said.

*

Just after though, considered
to have a tendency
of which he'd been ignorant,
all he could do was listen,

fearful he'd make his rhythm
jag by the fervency
with which he wished it wouldn't.

Pretty Bird

He bought her a gift at the doldrum beginnings
of what turned out to be an illness
but then just seemed malaise, the blues—
a mynah bird for company,
black as a wing of Asian hair,
the little bill, a wedge of sun,
gem bits of amber eyes that shone
with otherly intelligence.
Not that she'd need the company,
he planned to take the overdue
retirement; they loved the Ventnor house.
Now they could be around it more,
good company as ever, the two
for each other, and now also
for Mr. McCaw, the name she chose.

He joked that he'd been tempted by
a parrot as better suiting the parlor's
décor—and parlor was the word—
but mynahs, too, were fashionable
in her century of preference.
He'd tease about Victoriana,
how mesmerized by the red and blue
Orientalia of the carpet,
someday they'd fall into the clutches
of clawfoot chairs and be devoured.

And what with *horror vacui*,
space lavished in small increments
on knickknacks, plant stands, cameos,
where would they ever find the room
for the bird in that room,
                              which more and more
she'd kept to—during those low weeks
before the pain, the doctors, the tests?
After, when they could do nothing really
but make her comfortable in parlor,
bedroom, bed—Mr. McCaw
was everywhere her chief distraction.
Her husband daily blessed the mynah,
wept sometimes with gratitude
for her to have the intervals
of joy at the lateral dance on the perch,
the blink-quick jab and jerk of his head
as she tried teaching him to talk
while she had strength to sit upright.
O hail to thee Mr. McCaw,
you pretty bird, Hello McCaw—
talking and talking to make him talk
till talk he did, his own name only
for the longest time, cawing McCaw,
and then he turned impressionist:
her dear voice calling for her husband,
cheery as it was for a while,
then cracked and weakened, then restored—
times shuffled and played at random:
the laughter of two months ago,
a sudden birdy shriek of pain,
her sung-out greeting she's awake,
come in, when she so clearly wasn't,

couldn't be, the hospice nurse's
name in a moan, the thump of heels
rushing from the kitchen hallway,
the mynah's only sound effect,
the rest—voiced or breathed—hers,
all of it, sounds she made trying
to live except for one, which was
the sound her dying made in her,
which also passed into the bird,
into the repertoire, death rattle,
so-called, more a candle guttering
audibly down in its waxy juices,
shuddering out the light of her
last breath, that ragged purr, over
and over after all was over—
no telling when.
               No telling what
would come at any time, no knowing
what voice of hers would summon him
and to which precinct of his grief.

Busying himself around the house
tensed for the strike of memory—
through the medium of McCaw,
he heard himself saying out loud—
though not McCaw as medium,
bringing her message from beyond
the grave, surely nothing like that
in those fragments of endearments.
If something spoke out of the atom
of obsession in the bird, he felt
a message from the universe
itself he almost understood,

broadcast haphazardly, received
by chance, vaguely concerning fate.
He didn't know how things should end, though.
What was sufficient as the natural
cost of loving anything?
He'd keep McCaw until the bird
learned his last breath to add to hers.

His doctor and some friends came by,
meaning him to hear her voice
in theirs: what she would want for him,
persuading him to let them take
the bird to someone who would board
the mynah for him, let him visit,
or, if he wanted, take it back.
Allowing himself to be persuaded,
he sent McCaw away and brought
him home within a week that time,
returned him then, then took him back.
This, then, would be the pattern, to
and fro, of his remaining life.

One day he opened up the cage,
intending to take McCaw in his hands
for what purpose he hardly knew.
It occurred to him the very fingers
that could block the beak's pinprick
nostrils would simply register
the trilling heart as he'd hold McCaw
a moment in one hand cupped
and cradled against his own heart,
and with the other raise the window
and hand the bird out to the air

to find his way to join the other
exotics in their colonies,
thriving year round in northern cities.
He'd seen the pictures on the news:
trellised plumage, a floral-feathered
meadow sloped against some height,
on some abandoned industry,
the mesh and girders lively with launch
and landings—or a birdhouse of banks
of disused stadium loudspeakers—
parrots, parakeets, cockatiels,
their feathers trembled by the wind,
their trembling of the air with wings.
In the middle of the rookery din
of chatter and cheeping, whistle and song,
those who'd been taught to speak would speak.
McCaw would speak there—

is that you? . . .
God, my God . . . love, could you . . . pretty—
or having flown out to roost elsewhere,
the death sound become the slowing flutter
of wings, steadying him on the branch
or stanchion he's just landed on,
or it's a power line above
a street where knots of children play,
and he is saying over them—
dear, dearest hold me always.

The Man at the Art House

The art house, revival house, itself revived
three times, conceived first as a music hall,
shows foreign cinema and resurrects
American films, new when it was first renewed.
The one on screen three comes from the forties.
A decade for which the man in the tenth row
barely arrived in time. In his forties now,
he is weeping at the movie in which a man
also in his forties, though playing younger,
has moved the necessary distance through
the plot's too rough, too neat, approximations
of what might occur, to become the man returning.

The bus trip starts it: a small canvas satchel
held on his lap, the unsought conversation
with the nosey old fellow in the next seat,
the conversation he seeks with his old friend
who works at the garage near the bus stop,
for news of someone in this town where he'd lived,
not his hometown, though he wants to come home
to it, to the woman he thought interim,
an accommodation, love as a low point's refuge
and no more, not more surely, until it happened
to him, he happened on it elsewhere, the knowledge
that true as she was then, demanding then
so little, she wanted so much—not gratitude,

she had had gratitude—but love from him,
all he had to give, and more than that,
she deserved by virtue of her constancy,
her love, that gift, if she still wanted it.

And to feel all this! To be that man returning,
to be able to return with a whole heart,
healed somehow and then suddenly, though
everyone knows what's coming, the moment comes.
They sit in a kitchen of the period,
calico pattern on the table cloth,
the pattern of their speech, period, too:
Why show up now? Don't be such a mug.
His hand offered, taken, and released,
her movement away abrupt, getting up,
going to the window. His movement toward her—
the shot over his shoulder, over hers
as she turns at his hand's touch on her shoulder,
turning to him and into their embrace,
which signifies hearts given once again—
for it is a reprise of a sort for both of them
but given once and for all. To see all this
from his seat in the dark, close to the center aisle,
and even if then and only then to imagine
there is such a man, revenant, returning whole,
but to know that it is not him, never yet, never—
why, those are the tears of the man who watches the movie.

Vision

For the sad man, legally
blind in several states without
his glasses, who sits
on the side of the bed,
there comes a moment in a tear,
in the gathering
before the fall in the criss-
cross of forces and
resistances, an equipoise
between surface tension
and gravity and the thin
dam of the lower lid,
brimming but not
brimmed over yet,
and the mass becomes a shape,
the shape a lens that compensates
exactly for his deficit in seeing,
and he sees.
        He sees
his glasses cross-legged
on the nightstand, unblurred titles
on the spines of books lining
a sharp-edged shelf,
things standing clearly
as what they are
while he focuses away

on these present objects,
on this odd interval itself,
which is like some revelation—
as if before the tear falls
from his eyes scales might,
a moment like a moment
in which a vision comes,
except there is no vision,
only this form of it.

Air Over Fire

A friend of mine saw
from a building nearby,
      only he didn't know what
he was seeing,

thought it was debris.
His mind wouldn't permit
          otherwise,
no matter how sharp his eye.

It took a camera's quickness
and the next day's paper
      to convince him
with a bodily shock

that he had seen a man
who had chosen air over fire
      and jumped from that height
before it came down,

before people safe on side streets
threw up their hands,
      unable not to,
as the tower began to fall,

seeming to try to prevent
the cascading
          with their hands and cries,
to hold the towers up

as they would have borne up
the falling man—
          the man flying down,
for so he appeared

in the photograph,
his arms out,
          as if in choosing
the air,

he also chose to give himself
to a final pleasure,
          his face composed
for that instant in the perfect light.

Sacrifice

Baghdad c. 1995

Here is fire and wood for sacrifice, said Isaac, but where is the lamb . . . ?

The newscaster shows without much commentary
beyond that it was smuggled the video
of the dance the men of the desert cult perform

before the dictator and his family.
As absolute as any have ever been,
he sits in a standard wing chair in the palace,

less like a king, though, than a desert god
made visible as graven image, impassive—
the obsidian-eyed attentiveness revealed

in the almost averted gaze of the camera
as it wobbles after the dancers, passing him
and over patterns on a wall suggesting

calligraphy, as in the style of the region.
Easy to think the dance was made for him,
but he must have summoned them already aware

of the usual range of their improvisations
to that ancient city near the original places.
In fact the dance is older than the city

and ugly, the steps fierce but perfunctory,
done to keep the rhythm going of music
we cannot hear, that has not been recorded,

to which they seem to imitate, preempt
the famous cruelty: pierce themselves with daggers
and stakes through fleshy parts of their upper arms,

and onto a spot just above the hip
one shuffling man applies a pistol barrel,
and spins out of the frame with the jolt of the discharge.

Then they bring out the child and lay him down
and lay a blade across his naked belly—
but what cuts away suddenly is the tape,

leaving a black moment before the men
return bringing the boy with them, unhurt,
having danced what might be required, what has been,

by the great God or else some little ones
whose relevant texts are never texts alone,
but a scriptiform bramble in the midst of which,

after whoever is saved by whatever quirk
of grace, the rest are tangled, rams in the thicket.

Elegy

for Meyer Kopp

Death dissolved you sweetly,
grain by hourly grain,
till all that was left was sweetness,
till only your sweetness remained.

For eighty years, buying time,
you sent ahead what we all send:
your hair, your teeth, the slender ends
of fingernails, not minding

the losses any more than when
it was your dearest moments
you offered to oblivion.
As if the pages of an album

in one final turning, turned
in the currents of a fire,
gave up their scenes for burning—burned
your mother's kitchen, the harness shop

your father kept, head-down his side locks
swung to the hammer's tap. A choir
of village children in a line,
voices to whom you sing in answer,

suddenly surrendering
to the time the liveliest of dancers
chose you at a *landsleit* ball
remembered, remembering.

Forgetting then, forgotten all
the passing things that anger was,
releasing one by one to silence
the words of several languages,

the names you gave your children,
whose tender child at last you were,
taking less than you had been
therefore away from them forever,

sweetly, grain by grain,
till not even your sweetness remained.

The New People

*Their identity is a matter of conjecture: are they survivors of a tribal
battle, ostracized offenders of a village code, victims of a mental or
physical disease, or simply people who got lost and never found their
way home through the faceless jungle?*

—COUSTEAU AND RICHARDS

We'd come upriver through the zones of burning,
lands settlers seared into thin-skinned fields,
good only for grazing and only for a while.
Dug-out canoes and metal boats rocked
in our backwash.
                    Shore people stared us past:
lip disc of bone, plastic beads, stone adz,
machete, shotgun, blowgun, penis sheath,
rock band t-shirt—or chatted when we put in:
Arawakan, Spanish, Carib, Portuguese.

Then no one for weeks till huddled in the palms'
wide spaces on the riverbank, browner
than the bark, two women and a girl-child,
naked and unadorned, neither scar
nor ornament to signal who they were.
I fancied we looked edible to them,
the color of what's eaten elsewhere

at least—apple snail and manioc—
as we stripped off our clothes to demonstrate
that we also were human. They could approach
and speak to us.
                    But when at last they did,
it was like nothing anyone had heard,
and close to nothing, those few sounds of theirs,
even our genius of the region's tongues
could not decipher the words if they were words.
We held up fruit and flower, laid hands on trees,
pointed at a snake snaking past,
a question in our every motion, each sound
interrogatory. Still for anything
we would have wanted said, we could discover
no name among them.
                    We showed them fire, waving
fingers, hands like treetops in a whirlwind—
then fire amazing in a nest of branches.

Yet when they sat together that way they had,
seeming to touch even when they didn't,
you'd dream a forest where anything wanted
was in reach and given, offered before the asking,
even each other, covenant and precept,
utter, unuttered, made from proximity.

When did inquiry change into instruction
in our version of the barter they could make
forever after, gesture and speech, the trade
of name for thing, the name instead, the name
until the thing could come or be brought, what
to call, therefore to call and call? A fist,
thumb out, tilting down to the mouth means drink,

thirst—a hand scooping up: eat, hunger.
They managed a few signs and tried the sounds:
yes to our water to drink, yes to food,
no no they would not step onto the boat.
They took our gift of blankets but performed
refusal throwing them down, walking off,
and creeping back to take them up again.

We spoke of them as traumatized, a remnant
of a tribe. We thought: *massacre, plague*—and mimed,
tableau vivant, all manner of disaster,
dying to know what happened to the rest.
We stood a group of three exactly where
they stood when we had sighted them, one kneeling
on the right to be the child, till from their eyes
we felt for certain they knew we stood for them.
We then reset the scene so all of us
milled there among the palms, a stand-in tribe.
Then came subtraction, *tableau morte*, and all
were carried off in deathly variations
except the three alter originals
who occupied the space alone again.
The trio audience across the way,
who had appeared to us right here bewildered
days before, seemed now again bewildered,
looking at each other, looking at us,
until the one that we called Alma got up,
circulated urgently, staring
into our faces, giving her clearest signs,
the subject afterward of much discussion.
So many of us had trained to play at credence
of a kind, chattering "systems of belief,"
but how much language was the minimum

sufficient for beliefs?
                         We believed at least
that she did, that time before she could truly speak
in words we understood, believed enough
to bring us back to this part of the river
five years later to hear the halting words she had
by then—a Babel tongue of pidgin tongues,
for what she signaled at our pantomime—
the shrugs of her own or ones that we had taught
to her, the shaking of her head, *no*—
that she recalled no others because there were
no others to recall, that there had been
no dying before we came, that they emerged
at our beckoning entire, having been
no, not the last of all their kind but first.

Civilization

What you could call
its last outpost,
a place like that,
the absolute of frost,
too cold for snowfall,
the solitary shack,
barracks and lab and all,
which freak mischance blew flat
with everyone else lost,
along with stored supplies—
almost as entirely
as if the ice
had gaped and swallowed,

except what sealed doom was the fiery
propane blast that followed—
as if the sacrifice
had proved acceptable,
he wrote in his diary,
scrawling in the shallow
crater where he sheltered
in a lean-to in the rubble
that hardly filtered
wind. Using body heat,
carefully he'd melted
a little drinking water.

That the radio stayed dead
despite his fiddling didn't matter,
the fierceness of the weather
enough to make
rescue impossible
for several weeks,
when others would shiver as they read
entries about the penguins,
the ones he planned to take:
of which only the second
would have been for him to eat
he swore, the first for friend.
He needed just to calculate
a way to keep it fed.

The Man Who Sleeps in My Office

The radio not quite on my station and up
too high, faint traces of a cologne's large scent,
strongest in the fabric of the couch—
indents in the arm and cushion and in them
the tight wound tiny curls of hair I first thought
fell from my body: the smallest disarrangements,
still telling, nonetheless, more and more
deducibles, the evidence, a trail.

So if I had the thought, half-thought, dream-thought,
the only presences in this old building
were the dead, I was awakened by
a live one who sleeps in my office, I'm convinced,
who occupies these spaces only when
I don't, who is supposed to pick up trash
if I have thrown it down, to empty the waste-
baskets and dust the shelves of the dust, that is,
I've read, partly the erosions of my skin,
who is supposed to, but frequently does not.
Among the things he does do regularly,
judging by signs he leaves behind, is sleep.

And he seems clever, clever enough perhaps
to hold two jobs by stealing sleep here
and there on each, to work just fast enough
and just enough to gather time for sleep

and whatever else he does with time, clever
enough to gauge the limits of what I'd do
to make him stop. He may be wrong, however.
I left word with the elderly night watchman
who has business here some afternoons
of what I did not want and what I did.

The man is clever. What I lay on my couch
as obstruction: complex patterns of files and papers,
carefully devised, are reproduced
with subtle variations, a quiet trumping.
He specializes in these fugitive
displacements, tease of his inhabitation.
Nothing's missing, only moved, and seldom
far, though sometimes from the shelves to the shelves
across, a mirror-imaged spot, a book,
stapler, or calculator will be transported—
unless I have forgotten where they started,
but I don't think I could forget so much.

When little broken springs of hair appeared
embedded in the close weave of the jacket
I keep here and on the collar of the spare shirt,
I went to his supervisor with a speech
in which I made it clear that while I wanted
nothing bad to happen to the man—
I thought he might have been "taking his break,"
lying down during his lunch hour
in my office in the middle of the night,
but maybe he could take it somewhere else.
The supervisor more than sympathized.
He turns out to be the practiced sort of boor
who stops just short of using words for others

that would tell too much of what he is himself:
he says, *these people, they, how they are*—adding
cleaners, damn night crew, the whole bunch.
I say I can't be sure and call him off
for now. He lets me know what it will mean
if I should come to him again, and that
I only have to come to him again.

Meanwhile, I build my case out of the spatters
in the microwave that I don't recognize,
small stains on the couch, drips on the rug.
Sometimes when I spill, I will admit,
I'll tell one whom I tell, a colleague in whom
I've confided about the man, the stain is the man's.
On the desk top, the strange Semitic script
of hair I'll find when I'm alone, which dropped
likely from me, I'll say to myself is his.

Nights working late I've sensed him on his way,
although I never managed staying long
enough to see him. Welling up beneath
me once or twice, most often coming down
from floors above, I have made out the bass line
of his music. He plays it loud, no one
he knows around to hear. I've felt it in
my middle more than heard before I went.

I leave him notes, no need for address of course
of either sort, no opening salutation,
no close, the simple text of my request—
(more civil than reminders I leave myself:
take such-and-such a file, call so-and-so)
asking forbearance in captions—laid on, leaned on,

or affixed to objects as if it were their speech:
please do not lie here, please do not use this,
please do not move. I find the notes themselves
moved, inched over right or left, rotated
a few degrees—he must handle them to read.

He is a reader as I am—although
his tastes run to works of faith, the Bible
and books that comment on its mysteries.
I know because I've answered his trespass
with trespass of my own. I found his closet
beneath the first floor stairs, the wingspread book
nesting on dried rags and folded bags
on a corner shelf beside a metal sink,
a Bible, cracked open at *Revelation*, pages
of passages underlined—stacked books
on prophecy in a doorless cupboard—scattered
on the floor, magazines with articles
about times near the end, the mailing labels'
many names from every part of town.

I will stay later than I ever stayed,
wait as long as need be, as he drifts down
like ash or paper falling in a place
of static air, swinging side to side,
office to office, criss-crossing corridors,
down from the heights to settle here like a bird
or bat or moth. When I can feel his music,
at first descending through the upper floors
as I have done before, then, through the wall,
big bass throbbing like the heart of elsewhere
pulsing me, I promise not to leave,
not to measure time by any other task

than waiting here to meet him face to face
when each can ask the other for what he wants
and each can say what he can do or can't.

Man Aboard

He woke up two years later, assuming
in the shock of his discovery
that so much time had passed
without his consciousness

that he must have seemed to others
non compos, that he would have been
put away, put by, but there he was,
traveling from his den

to the living room
where the television and the paper, *The Times*,
on the coffee table, tended to confirm
what came to him minutes before

as he sat peering down at a wrist watch
of the sort that gives out date with time,
registering no extremity of amazement,
just a natural coming to,

and when he came to, what he came to
as he moved out into the house
greeting the people there,
none of whom shouted for joy

or with amazement—recalled to life—
his daughters looked up from screen and page,
or rather one did and smiled,
the other too intent on what she was doing,

his wife, passing through,
raised an eyebrow
in that way she had of inviting words
from others, a tic he'd once said

of expectancy—a little bemused,
he himself had to restrain
no impulse to whoop
at his own restoration,

yet who else would?—
since what he came to
with certainty was that
he hadn't been missed during his absence,

had seemed much the same
as always he did
when he remembered
he was present and was present,

or recalled he'd not been
after some distracted seconds,
he simply knew he had betrayed
no sign of his own disappearance,

had occupied the time
doing his intricate calculations
at work, and at home: at the table
peeling an orange for the girls

in a single pending strip,
even in the marriage bed,
not giving it away
in any respect that he was gone.

Legion

There are a number of us in here, one of whom
apparently wanted to remember something
the others didn't, but he doesn't know what
and stands in the middle of the room at a loss.

A pen behind the ear, perhaps it had to do with paper
(it's been paper before), a notebook, some kind of ledger,
or a single sheet or scrap with information on it
concerning . . . I don't know what—I don't remember.

He is looking for it, though. He's the one
who wanders the deserted rooms positively
Jewish in his fatalistic resignation, and in
many other ways, he reminds himself, catching
sight of Ginzberg's *Legends of the Jews*
in a bookshelf packed with Judaica.

The people of the book aside, the people—
other, outward, actual—who live here also,
not in at the moment, have left evidence: shoes,
glasses in the sink, a coat—arms wide, gaping its flat
flung-back exhaustion on the couch.

Outside his head and inside, people:
wife, sons, daughter—two handsome
red-headed women, two strapping lads.

Might it be he has reasons not to remember,
something on the paper suggesting betrayal,
an unpaid bill, an uncalled number, an ad
for some foolish thing he longs to buy tantamount
to an admission that life is insufficient as it is?

So whenever it was, whoever I was that set down
the scrap or page, receding just for now—
not vanishing, surely he'll return—
has taken with him the memory of where,

leaving the rest of us to act out of our
imperative, a faith, steadfast if anxious,
that the paper has importance as does
therefore the life around it—
so we search for it and for the reason
it got lost, though neither discovery
would be enough to proof
us against such losses as may come in any moment.

Crow of the Galápagos

The blackest crow in all the Galápagos
and his brethren, also, whittle now
with their beaks,
                            shaping the thorny twigs
of a native bush, until it is unrecognizable
any longer as a twig from a bush,

until it has been turned into a tool
with which to plunge into holes after insects.

We have known for years that in the time after
our failure,
                            prepared for during the time of our failure,
there would be others to come after us.

And so the crows come, finding merit in logic,
and the legion of the cockroach, unextirpatable,
and the sum total of the ants and bees—

all of whom we have mistreated,
all of whom measure us:
                                        for piercing
with thorns, for poison, for the simple crush,
from whom we can expect no mercy

when they are ready to descend from the wide sky
or teem up from beneath,
as perdurable vermin as we have been.

Lines, in the Reflexive

Say a writer imagines something horrible
for a character, unspeakable as
a severed tongue, or worse,

and renders it in a story, a story
or a poem, and a reader, mad and childlike,
reads it, lies in wait for the writer

and does to him what he did
to his character.
What to make of this unpoetic injustice,

and who has done it? Who is author
of the eventual deed? The doer
in extremis and alone and none else?

Must it alter the case if it were
the writer himself, not himself, leaving himself
behind in a madness, making of himself

the exact sort of victim he has made
of his character, altering his own flesh?
And whatever can be the motive beyond

a rage for the symmetrical
standing in for God?
And why must I think of this,

and if I've thought of this
or something like, what have I unleashed
on me or into the world?

Pylon Man

Bone self, a self gone down
to the bone, stick figure
who'd be a diagram of force,
vector of blast, the legs' wide angle,
and on your feet, a pylon man.

Who thinks you this? Not you—
wanting to leave a mark
on the world with a life
become the sole desire.
The heavy hum atop in the high wires
starts climbing the pitches.

A mark, a mark,
but not flyspeck,
not blood prints of the head of a bird,
no more than a frantic heart with wings,
battered on wall and window,

but to take the wall and window with you,
and, if not the house,
then the ridiculous thin wall of skin
between you and them,
between you and the world—

girdled round with what will take
the outside in and through,
all the compass points through each other
on their way out
to nothing, to making a nonsense
of outside and inside,

to abolish and thereby to establish,
to put a root down in memory
anyone might stumble on,
even after others have forgotten,
even after those who must remember
as long as they live are gone—

to comprehend the world as a blinding flash,
to think of several persons in it precisely
over and over as you prepare
to fix the bodies' places in outline,
in shadow on a wall.

What does it mean that I think I know
what someone feels on the way to breaking
and the breaking of others,
I, who climb down always from the ledge
of any departure,
I, who prefer the quiet flame in the guts
over the bursting star of them?

The Dog I'll Never Own

snorts in a dream, as he sleeps at my feet
in a winter-brisk office near a glowing heater.

First it was my parents' fault, always promising
to move to places dogs were allowed

and never doing it, and now it is mine:
for the love I do not have for him

I will give up the love I might have had from him.
He may well be a Rhodesian Ridgeback,

the muscle moving like another animal
beneath the thin skin, who would circle

and circle me if I were an intruder—
these hyena habits marking him

as surely as the stripe of hair down his back
running contrary to the lie of the rest.

I am more accustomed to what I've had from cats
I will not own, as they slide pleasingly close

on their way elsewhere, and me on mine.
The dog pulls at his leash, wants us on our way

together, sniffs at the path for the story, stops, growls
at some heavyish stir in the underbrush,

which he knows cannot be me, still he looks back
to see if I am the cause, if I am

throwing stones, but how could I deceive him,
when his grave eyes seek mine for the moment

he permits himself before he looks
away? And even had it been a trick,

it wouldn't have been for my amusement
but to test his skill—he can sense the joy

I take in his accomplishments.
He swings his head toward the place of the sound

and tugs again, ready to go forward
without me, yet on my behalf,

to begin the arc of his inspection outward
and return, or to corral in shrinking

concentricities something out there,
though nothing is out there now.

So I release him from the tether,
and the collar, anywhere he goes

because he wants to is what I want
from him now, for I am done

with the thousand things he would do,
easy to imagine, and other things, one

in the stillness of communion, lying where
he would lie, unsayable in the ordinary ways.

The Long Flight Almost Over

So much circling near the end
     of the long flight,
         nearer to calamity than we knew
until the first equivocal announcement
that gasped whispers greeted,
     sweeping the rows, and a few scattered cries.

Then suddenly those of us
     who had taken off our shoes—
         the dozen soldiers in stocking feet,
a few who lay over vacant seats had to be
         roused to buckle in—
had no time to put them on again,

and women in heels had to take theirs off anyway
along with jewelry—
         and me my eyeglasses,
to slip into the seat pocket in front of me.
     Everyone either braced
         against the forward seat back

or hinged shut, chest to lap, arms around knees.
The brother-stranger with whom
     I hadn't spoken

              reached across the empty
middle seat to clasp
        my left hand with his right,

and then we retracted and reclenched,
descending steeply to the pilot's
              drawled deadpan optimism
                      again about the landing gear—
how we had to take precautions.
Probably just the warning light,

                      but it wasn't.
Shrieks then, of metal, too,
              as we touched down and tipped,
                      grinding the runway,
bags breaking out of overhead bins,
shoes tumbling down the aisles.

We'd surged to the doors in stumbling lines
        and slid the yellow vinyl chutes,
              to wade clouds of foam laid down for the fire
that hadn't come,
        to be bussed to the terminal lounge,
              to wait for our things, and for the people

who had waited for us on the ground.
Even among those embracing there,
        you could meet a pair of eyes
              over a shoulder or to the side,
our naked faces presented to each other,
the gaze held so long, never longer outside of love—

until the faint slow smile,
a closing of the eyes, or the look away.
A group of soldiers in a corner still sorted
their gleaming patent leather shoes,
difficult to find whose
were whose in the common heap.

His Mother Calling

He wonders it disturbs him as it does,
her running through a little list of names
before she comes to his, and he's right there
in front of her, it's him she's been attempting
to address (although he's heard her do it, calling
from another room), but she begins
to say his father's name, her brother's name—
a quick ratchet through first consonants
at best, or a stuttered switch of syllables
in trial before she ends where she intended.

Mostly it seems to happen without occasion,
though worse he thinks when she is tired or flustered.
It's not that he's been talking on and she
must say his name to get her say at all,
but just the ordinary emphasis
that has her stumbling through his father's name,
her brother's name, though maybe he's been teasing,
some wise-guy patter like her brother's, which might
account for how that name came into it.

Big families he could understand. A friend
of his, the middle child of seven, says
his mother always sounds like she's reciting
Bible genealogy at speed
from fragmentary texts—*Oh Ad-uh No*

Jay Beh David. But here with three all told,
as nuclear as it gets, what's going on?
She couldn't be unsure of who he is?

Well, something's looser held than he would want
in the person he takes after, no matter what
they say about him looking like his father,
a sign of where the taking after leads,
or else the knowledge to which she summons him
with his father's name, her brother's name, might be
less preview than reminder—that he was not
the only one, that he was not the first.

The Voices

At the limit of the power
to resist are the voices—
on the border in between
sleeping and waking
anyone may hear them
on that rare occasion
painlessly, or at the verges
past exhaustion's
fluent imagery.

Sometimes an old man
will hear them
unmuffled by
the beating of his heart,
at first thinking
they are specially for him:
the beloved come round again,
some few he'd injured
seeking their redress.

Beyond all that
and for any who can manage
passing by,
the voices, themselves, drift
unparticular as sirens,
their address not even air.